Our Holidays

Celebrate Hanukkah

Elizabeth Lawrence

Cavendish Square
New York

Published in 2016 by Cavendish Square Publishing, LLC
243 5th Avenue, Suite 136, New York, NY 10016

Copyright © 2016 by Cavendish Square Publishing, LLC

First Edition

CPSIA Compliance Information: Batch #WS15CSQ

All websites were available and accurate when this book was sent to press.

Library of Congress Cataloging-in-Publication Data

Lawrence, Elizabeth, 1988– author.
Celebrating Hanukkah / Elizabeth Lawrence.
pages cm. — (Our holidays)
Includes index.
ISBN 978-1-50260-410-1 (hardcover)
ISBN 978-1-50260-409-5 (paperback)
ISBN 978-1-50260-411-8 (ebook)
1. Hanukkah. I. Title.

BM695.H3L366 2015
296.4'35—dc23

2014049165

Editorial Director: David McNamara
Editor: Kristen Susienka
Copy Editor: Cynthia Roby
Art Director: Jeffrey Talbot
Designer: Joseph Macri
Senior Production Manager: Jennifer Ryder-Talbot
Production Editor: Renni Johnson

The photographs in this book are used by permission and through the courtesy of: Michele Westmorland/Getty Images, Cover; Bushnell/Soifer/The Image Bank/Getty Images, 5; Robert Nicholas/OJO Images/Getty Images, 7; kali9/E+/Getty Images, 9; Pam Ostrow/Getty Images, 11; Noam Armonn/Shutterstock.com, 13; © iStockphoto.com/sbossert, 15; Fuse/Getty Images, 17; Lisa F. Young/Shutterstock.com, 19; Fuse/Getty Images, 21.

Printed in the United States of America

Contents

Hanukkah is a special holiday.

It is eight days long and takes place in November or December.

5

At Hanukkah we remember a group of people called the **Maccabees**.

The Maccabees won a war. This let them pray in a building called a **temple**.

7

Today we celebrate Hanukkah with family and friends.

9

A **menorah** is an important symbol of Hanukkah.

People light a candle on the menorah every day of Hanukkah.

11

People sing songs, too.

13

Families and friends eat food together.

Potato pancakes with applesauce and sour cream are favorite Hanukkah foods.

15

Games are also fun.

Dreidel is one game to play at Hanukkah.

People give chocolate that looks like gold coins at Hanukkah.

18

Hanukkah is a fun holiday!

20

New Words

dreidel (DRAY-del) A four-sided object that spins on its tip. Each side has a letter on it.

Maccabees (MAK-ka-beez) A group of people living many years ago in what is now Israel.

menorah (me-NO-ruh) A nine-stemmed candle holder used at Hanukkah.

temple (TEM-pull) A building where people prayed.

Index

About the Author

Elizabeth Lawrence lives in Albany, New York. She likes to write books, celebrate holidays with family and friends, and cook.

About

Bookworms help independent readers gain reading confidence through high-frequency words, simple sentences, and strong picture/text support. Each book explores a concept that helps children relate what they read to the world in which they live.